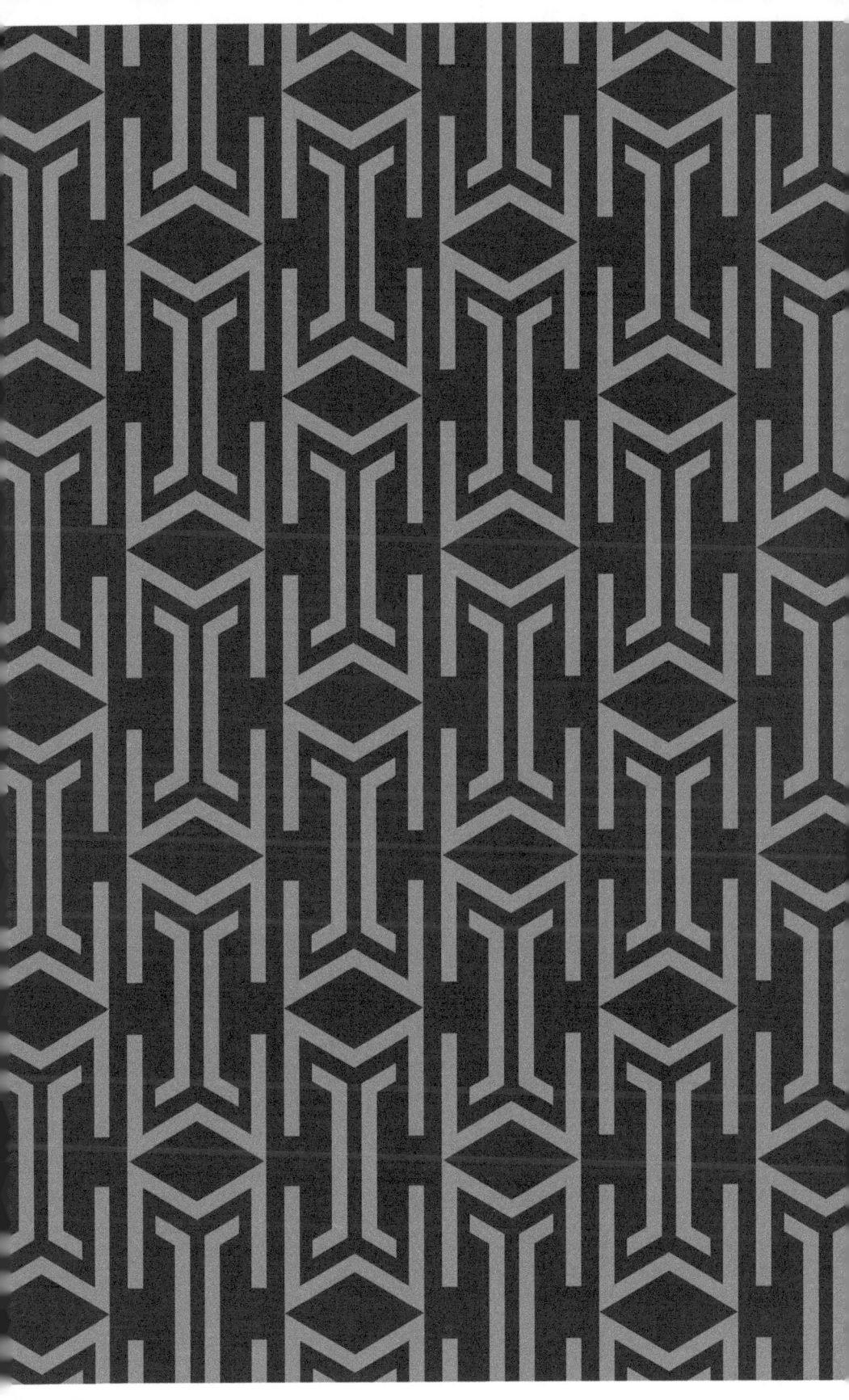

ISBN 978-1-7359624-2-9

Made2Thrive Success Planner is published by Integrity Center in Lincoln, Nebraska

MADE2THRIVE

PERSONAL SUCCESS PLANNER

CREATE A STRATEGIC PLAN FOR LIFE

USE **MADE2THRIVE'S** 4 PILLARS

ENJOY THE JOURNEY OF SUCCESS

NAME_____

EMAIL_____

PHONE_____

YEAR_____ QUARTER ○ ○ ○ ○

GET STARTED

The *Made2Thrive Personal Success Planner* is designed to help you live your mission, achieve your goals and life vision.

1   **BEGIN YOUR PLANNER**. Fill in the first week or two of daily pages.

2   **WRITE YOUR MISSION AND VISION**. Clearly define your goals and use your daily pages to help make your mission and vision a reality.

3   **TAKE TIME EVERY DAY TO SET YOURSELF UP FOR SUCCESS**. Choose your 3 Daily Thrive Actions or to-do's and write in your meetings each day.

4   **KEEP YOUR PLANNER WITH YOU AT ALL TIMES**. Use it as the tool that it's meant to be.

To help you get started, please take some time to watch these videos at **Made2Thri e.live/gettingstarted**

Please share the *Made2Thrive Personal Success Planner* with others by forwarding the link to our site (**Made2Thrive.live/products**).

Now would be a great time to order your next planner as well so you will have it ready to go at the end of this quarter as you do your *quarterly review* and *preview.*

MISSION STATEMENT

When crafting your *mission* statement, ask yourself the following:

WHAT DO YOU ENJOY DOING? _____

_____

_____

_____

_____

_____

WHAT ARE YOU PASSIONATE ABOUT? _____

_____

_____

_____

_____

_____

WHAT GIVES YOU PURPOSE? _____

_____

_____

_____

_____

_____

WHAT GIVES YOU JOY IN YOUR LIFE? _____

_____

_____

_____

_____

WHAT MOTIVATES YOU TO GET OUT OF BED EACH MORNING?

_____

_____

_____

_____

_____

_____

MISSION STATEMENT

MY MISSION STATEMENT (version 1)

My mission is _____

_____

_____

_____

_____

_____

MY MISSION STATEMENT (version 2)

My mission is _____

_____

_____

_____

_____

_____

YOUR FINAL MISSION STATEMENT

_____

_____

_____

_____

_____

_____

MISSION STATEMENT EXAMPLE

"My mission is to help improve the lives of others by serving them with great passion."

— Tony Ojeda

VISION STATEMENT (PART 1)

When crafting your *vision* statement, ask yourself the following:

WHAT DO YOU SEE FOR YOUR FUTURE? _____
_____
_____
_____
_____
_____
_____

WHAT MATTERS MOST TO YOU? _____
_____
_____
_____
_____
_____
_____

WHAT DO YOU WANT YOUR PERFECT LIFE TO LOOK LIKE?
_____
_____
_____
_____
_____
_____

WHAT IS IT THAT YOU WANT TO DO? _____
_____
_____
_____
_____
_____

WHAT THINGS DO YOU WANT TO HAVE? _____
_____
_____
_____
_____

VISION STATEMENT (PART 2)

When writing your vision for each of the six life domains, fill in the statement below:

When I am _____ (age) I will …

SPIRITUAL

_____

_____

_____

_____

_____

_____

_____

_____

_____

_____

_____

_____

_____

RELATIONAL

_____

_____

_____

_____

_____

_____

_____

_____

_____

_____

_____

_____

_____

VISION STATEMENT (PART 2)

When writing your vision for each of the six life domains, fill in the statement below:
When I am _____ (age) I will …

FINANCIAL

_____

_____

_____

_____

_____

_____

_____

_____

_____

_____

_____

PHYSICAL

_____

_____

_____

_____

_____

_____

_____

_____

_____

_____

_____

_____

VISION STATEMENT (PART 2)

When writing your vision for each of the six life domains, fill in the statement below:
When I am _____ (age) I will …

PROFESSIONAL

_____
_____
_____
_____
_____
_____
_____
_____
_____
_____
_____
_____
_____
_____

PERSONAL

_____
_____
_____
_____
_____
_____
_____
_____
_____
_____
_____
_____
_____

ANNUAL GOALS

✓	#	Write your annual goals here.	Qtr.

ANNUAL GOALS

✓	#	Write your annual goals here.	Qtr.

GOAL DETAILS

Write your goal.　　　　　　　　　　　○ ACHIEVEMENT GOAL　　　○ HABIT GOAL

Domain　　○ SPIRITUAL　　　○ FINANCIAL　　　○ PROFESSIONAL
　　　　　　○ RELATIONAL　　○ PHYSICAL　　　○ PERSONAL

MY MOTIVATIONS / Write why these are important to you.

ACTION STEPS / List the best actions steps to get you closer to this goal.

CELEBRATE / Write down how you will celebrate when you achieve your goal.

GOAL DETAILS

Write your goal. ○ ACHIEVEMENT GOAL ○ HABIT GOAL

Domain
- ○ SPIRITUAL
- ○ RELATIONAL
- ○ FINANCIAL
- ○ PHYSICAL
- ○ PROFESSIONAL
- ○ PERSONAL

MY MOTIVATIONS / Write why these are important to you.

ACTION STEPS / List the best actions steps to get you closer to this goal.

CELEBRATE / Write down how you will celebrate when you achieve your goal.

GOAL DETAILS

Write your goal. ○ ACHIEVEMENT GOAL ○ HABIT GOAL

Domain ○ SPIRITUAL ○ FINANCIAL ○ PROFESSIONAL
          ○ RELATIONAL ○ PHYSICAL ○ PERSONAL

MY MOTIVATIONS / Write why these are important to you.

ACTION STEPS / List the best actions steps to get you closer to this goal.

CELEBRATE / Write down how you will celebrate when you achieve your goal.

GOAL DETAILS

Write your goal.　　　　　　　　　　　　○ ACHIEVEMENT GOAL　　　○ HABIT GOAL

Domain　　　○ SPIRITUAL　　　　○ FINANCIAL　　　　○ PROFESSIONAL
　　　　　　　○ RELATIONAL　　　○ PHYSICAL　　　　　○ PERSONAL

MY MOTIVATIONS / Write why these are important to you.

ACTION STEPS / List the best actions steps to get you closer to this goal.

CELEBRATE / Write down how you will celebrate when you achieve your goal.

GOAL DETAILS

Write your goal.   ○ ACHIEVEMENT GOAL   ○ HABIT GOAL

_____

_____

_____

_____

Domain   ○ SPIRITUAL   ○ FINANCIAL   ○ PROFESSIONAL

           ○ RELATIONAL   ○ PHYSICAL   ○ PERSONAL

MY MOTIVATIONS / Write why these are important to you.

ACTION STEPS / List the best actions steps to get you closer to this goal.

CELEBRATE / Write down how you will celebrate when you achieve your goal.

GOAL DETAILS

Write your goal.   ○ ACHIEVEMENT GOAL   ○ HABIT GOAL

Domain

○ SPIRITUAL   ○ FINANCIAL   ○ PROFESSIONAL

○ RELATIONAL   ○ PHYSICAL   ○ PERSONAL

MY MOTIVATIONS / Write why these are important to you.

ACTION STEPS / List the best actions steps to get you closer to this goal.

CELEBRATE / Write down how you will celebrate when you achieve your goal.

GOAL DETAILS

Write your goal.　　　　　　　　　　　　　○ **ACHIEVEMENT GOAL**　　　○ **HABIT GOAL**

Domain　　○ SPIRITUAL　　　○ FINANCIAL　　　○ PROFESSIONAL
　　　　　　○ RELATIONAL　　　○ PHYSICAL　　　○ PERSONAL

MY MOTIVATIONS / Write why these are important to you.

ACTION STEPS / List the best actions steps to get you closer to this goal.

CELEBRATE / Write down how you will celebrate when you achieve your goal.

GOAL DETAILS

Write your goal. ○ ACHIEVEMENT GOAL ○ HABIT GOAL

Domain
○ SPIRITUAL ○ FINANCIAL ○ PROFESSIONAL
○ RELATIONAL ○ PHYSICAL ○ PERSONAL

MY MOTIVATIONS / Write why these are important to you.

ACTION STEPS / List the best actions steps to get you closer to this goal.

CELEBRATE / Write down how you will celebrate when you achieve your goal.

GOAL DETAILS

Write your goal.   ○ **ACHIEVEMENT GOAL**   ○ **HABIT GOAL**

_____

_____

_____

_____

_____

Domain
  ○ SPIRITUAL   ○ FINANCIAL   ○ PROFESSIONAL
  ○ RELATIONAL   ○ PHYSICAL   ○ PERSONAL

MY MOTIVATIONS / Write why these are important to you.

ACTION STEPS / List the best actions steps to get you closer to this goal.

CELEBRATE / Write down how you will celebrate when you achieve your goal.

GOAL DETAILS

Write your goal.   ○ ACHIEVEMENT GOAL   ○ HABIT GOAL

Domain   ○ SPIRITUAL   ○ FINANCIAL   ○ PROFESSIONAL

○ RELATIONAL   ○ PHYSICAL   ○ PERSONAL

MY MOTIVATIONS / Write why these are important to you.

ACTION STEPS / List the best actions steps to get you closer to this goal.

CELEBRATE / Write down how you will celebrate when you achieve your goal.

GOAL DETAILS

Write your goal.   ○ **ACHIEVEMENT GOAL**   ○ **HABIT GOAL**

Domain   ○ SPIRITUAL   ○ FINANCIAL   ○ PROFESSIONAL
            ○ RELATIONAL   ○ PHYSICAL   ○ PERSONAL

MY MOTIVATIONS / Write why these are important to you.

ACTION STEPS / List the best actions steps to get you closer to this goal.

CELEBRATE / Write down how you will celebrate when you achieve your goal.

GOAL DETAILS

Write your goal.　　　　　　　　　　　○ ACHIEVEMENT GOAL　　　○ HABIT GOAL

Domain　　○ SPIRITUAL　　　○ FINANCIAL　　　○ PROFESSIONAL
　　　　　　○ RELATIONAL　　　○ PHYSICAL　　　○ PERSONAL

MY MOTIVATIONS / Write why these are important to you.

ACTION STEPS / List the best actions steps to get you closer to this goal.

CELEBRATE / Write down how you will celebrate when you achieve your goal.

PERFECT WEEK

WHAT WOULD YOUR PERFECT WEEK LOOK LIKE?

TIME	MONDAY	TUESDAY	WEDNESDAY
5:00 - 5:30			
5:30 - 6:00			
6:00 - 6:30			
6:30 - 7:00			
7:00 - 7:30			
7:30 - 8:00			
8:00 - 8:30			
8:30 - 9:00			
9:00 - 9:30			
9:30 - 10:00			
10:00 - 10:30			
10:30 - 11:00			
11:00 - 11:30			
11:30 - 12:00			
12:00 - 12:30			
12:30 - 1:00			
1:00 - 1:30			
1:30 - 2:00			
2:00 - 2:30			
2:30 - 3:00			
3:00 - 3:30			
3:30 - 4:00			
4:00 - 4:30			
4:30 - 5:00			
5:00 - 5:30			
5:30 - 6:00			
6:00 - 6:30			
6:30 - 7:00			
7:00 - 7:30			
7:30 - 8:00			
8:00 - 8:30			
8:30 - 9:00			

PERFECT WEEK

THURSDAY	FRIDAY	SATURDAY	SUNDAY

WEEKLY PREVIEW

VISION / Review your *vision* to help you remember what you want to accomplish in your six life domains.

QUARTERLY GOAL REVIEW / Write down the goals that you are focused on this quarter.

Goal 1: _____

_____

_____

    Next Action Steps:

    _____

    _____

    _____

    _____

Goal 2: _____

_____

_____

    Next Action Steps:

    _____

    _____

    _____

    _____

Goal 3: _____

_____

_____

    Next Action Steps:

    _____

    _____

    _____

    _____

WEEKLY PREVIEW

3 WEEKLY THRIVE ACTIONS / Write out the most important steps to help you move closer to your goals this week.

Action 1: _____
_____
_____

Action 2: _____
_____
_____

Action 3: _____
_____
_____

THIS WEEK AT A GLANCE / Write out any other personal or professional tasks that you have for this week.

PERSONAL
_____
_____
_____
_____
_____
_____

PROFESSIONAL
_____
_____
_____
_____
_____
_____

MONDAY

AGENDA | SCHEDULE

3 DAILY THRIVE ACTIONS
List the top 3 *to-do's* to get you closer to your goals.

○ _____

○ _____

○ _____

DAILY TASKS

DAILY TRIUMPHS

6 _____

7 _____

8 _____

9 _____

10 _____

11 _____

12 _____

1 _____

2 _____

3 _____

4 _____

5 _____

6 _____

7 _____

8 _____

DAILY NOTES

TUESDAY

AGENDA | SCHEDULE

3 DAILY THRIVE ACTIONS

List the top 3 *to-do's* to get you closer to your goals.

○ _____

○ _____

○ _____

DAILY TASKS

DAILY TRIUMPHS

6 _____

7 _____

8 _____

9 _____

10 _____

11 _____

12 _____

1 _____

2 _____

3 _____

4 _____

5 _____

6 _____

7 _____

8 _____

DAILY NOTES

WEDNESDAY

AGENDA | SCHEDULE

3 DAILY THRIVE ACTIONS

List the top 3 *to-do's* to get you closer to your goals.

○ _____

○ _____

○ _____

DAILY TASKS

DAILY TRIUMPHS

6 _____

7 _____

8 _____

9 _____

10 _____

11 _____

12 _____

1 _____

2 _____

3 _____

4 _____

5 _____

6 _____

7 _____

8 _____

DAILY NOTES

THURSDAY

AGENDA | SCHEDULE

3 DAILY THRIVE ACTIONS
List the top 3 *to-do's* to get you closer to your goals.

⭘ _____

⭘ _____

⭘ _____

DAILY TASKS

DAILY TRIUMPHS

6 _____

7 _____

8 _____

9 _____

10 _____

11 _____

12 _____

1 _____

2 _____

3 _____

4 _____

5 _____

6 _____

7 _____

8 _____

DAILY NOTES

FRIDAY

3 DAILY THRIVE ACTIONS
List the top 3 *to-do's* to get you closer to your goals.

○ _____

○ _____

○ _____

DAILY TASKS

DAILY TRIUMPHS

6 _____

7 _____

8 _____

9 _____

10 _____

11 _____

12 _____

1 _____

2 _____

3 _____

4 _____

5 _____

6 _____

7 _____

8 _____

DAILY NOTES

SATURDAY

AGENDA | SCHEDULE

3 DAILY THRIVE ACTIONS
List the top 3 *to-do's* to get you closer to your goals.

_____

◯ _____

◯ _____

◯ _____

_____

DAILY TASKS

DAILY TRIUMPHS

6 _____

7 _____

8 _____

9 _____

10 _____

11 _____

12 _____

1 _____

2 _____

3 _____

4 _____

5 _____

6 _____

7 _____

8 _____

DAILY NOTES

SUNDAY

AGENDA | SCHEDULE

3 DAILY THRIVE ACTIONS
List the top 3 *to-do's* to get you closer to your goals.

○ _____

○ _____

○ _____

DAILY TASKS

DAILY TRIUMPHS

6 _____

7 _____

8 _____

9 _____

10 _____

11 _____

12 _____

1 _____

2 _____

3 _____

4 _____

5 _____

6 _____

7 _____

8 _____

DAILY NOTES

WEEKLY REVIEW

STEP 1. BIGGEST TRIUMPHS / List your top accomplishments from the last week.

_____

_____

_____

_____

_____

_____

STEP 2. HOW FAR DID YOU GET ON YOUR 3 WEEKLY THRIVE ACTIONS?

_____

_____

_____

_____

_____

_____

STEP 3. WHAT WORKED AND WHAT DIDN'T?

_____

_____

_____

_____

_____

_____

STEP 4. MISSION STATEMENT REVIEW / Refer back to your _mission_. How well did you live out your _mission_ this past week? What do you need to do this week to better live out your _mission_?

_____

_____

_____

_____

_____

_____

"Weekly **reviews** help you reflect on
your previous week. Weekly **previews**
set you up for next week's success."

WEEKLY PREVIEW

VISION / Review your *vision* to help you remember what you want to accomplish in your six life domains.

QUARTERLY GOAL REVIEW / Write down the goals that you are focused on this quarter.

Goal 1: _____
_____
_____

    Next Action Steps:
    _____
    _____
    _____
    _____

Goal 2: _____
_____
_____

    Next Action Steps:
    _____
    _____
    _____
    _____

Goal 3: _____
_____
_____

    Next Action Steps:
    _____
    _____
    _____
    _____

WEEKLY PREVIEW

3 WEEKLY THRIVE ACTIONS / Write out the most important steps to help you move closer to your goals this week.

Action 1: _____

_____

_____

Action 2: _____

_____

_____

Action 3: _____

_____

_____

THIS WEEK AT A GLANCE / Write out any other personal or professional tasks that you have for this week.

PERSONAL

_____

_____

_____

_____

_____

_____

PROFESSIONAL

_____

_____

_____

_____

_____

_____

_____

MONDAY

AGENDA | SCHEDULE

3 DAILY THRIVE ACTIONS
List the top 3 *to-do's* to get you closer to your goals.

◯ _____

◯ _____

◯ _____

DAILY TASKS

DAILY TRIUMPHS

6 _____

7 _____

8 _____

9 _____

10 _____

11 _____

12 _____

1 _____

2 _____

3 _____

4 _____

5 _____

6 _____

7 _____

8 _____

DAILY NOTES

TUESDAY

AGENDA | SCHEDULE

3 DAILY THRIVE ACTIONS

List the top 3 *to-do's* to get you closer to your goals.

○ _____

○ _____

○ _____

DAILY TASKS

DAILY TRIUMPHS

6 _____

7 _____

8 _____

9 _____

10 _____

11 _____

12 _____

1 _____

2 _____

3 _____

4 _____

5 _____

6 _____

7 _____

8 _____

DAILY NOTES

WEDNESDAY

AGENDA | SCHEDULE

3 DAILY THRIVE ACTIONS
List the top 3 *to-do's* to get you closer to your goals.

○ _____

○ _____

○ _____

DAILY TASKS

DAILY TRIUMPHS

6 _____

7 _____

8 _____

9 _____

10 _____

11 _____

12 _____

1 _____

2 _____

3 _____

4 _____

5 _____

6 _____

7 _____

8 _____

DAILY NOTES

THURSDAY

AGENDA | SCHEDULE

3 DAILY THRIVE ACTIONS
List the top 3 *to-do's* to get you closer to your goals.

_____

◯ _____

◯ _____

◯ _____

_____

DAILY TASKS

DAILY TRIUMPHS

6 _____

7 _____

8 _____

9 _____

10 _____

11 _____

12 _____

1 _____

2 _____

3 _____

4 _____

5 _____

6 _____

7 _____

8 _____

DAILY NOTES

FRIDAY

AGENDA | SCHEDULE

3 DAILY THRIVE ACTIONS
List the top 3 *to-do's* to get you closer to your goals.

◯ _____

◯ _____

◯ _____

DAILY TASKS

DAILY TRIUMPHS

6 _____

7 _____

8 _____

9 _____

10 _____

11 _____

12 _____

1 _____

2 _____

3 _____

4 _____

5 _____

6 _____

7 _____

8 _____

DAILY NOTES

SATURDAY

AGENDA | SCHEDULE

3 DAILY THRIVE ACTIONS
List the top 3 *to-do's* to get you closer to your goals.

_____

◯ _____

◯ _____

◯ _____

DAILY TASKS

DAILY TRIUMPHS

6 _____

7 _____

8 _____

9 _____

10 _____

11 _____

12 _____

1 _____

2 _____

3 _____

4 _____

5 _____

6 _____

7 _____

8 _____

DAILY NOTES

SUNDAY

3 DAILY THRIVE ACTIONS

List the top 3 *to-do's* to get you closer to your goals.

○ _____

○ _____

○ _____

DAILY TASKS

DAILY TRIUMPHS

AGENDA | SCHEDULE

6 _____

7 _____

8 _____

9 _____

10 _____

11 _____

12 _____

1 _____

2 _____

3 _____

4 _____

5 _____

6 _____

7 _____

8 _____

DAILY NOTES

WEEKLY REVIEW

STEP 1. BIGGEST TRIUMPHS / List your top accomplishments from the last week.

_____

_____

_____

_____

_____

_____

STEP 2. HOW FAR DID YOU GET ON YOUR 3 WEEKLY THRIVE ACTIONS?

_____

_____

_____

_____

_____

_____

STEP 3. WHAT WORKED AND WHAT DIDN'T?

_____

_____

_____

_____

_____

_____

STEP 4. MISSION STATEMENT REVIEW / Refer back to your _mission_. How well did you live out your _mission_ this past week? What do you need to do this week to better live out your _mission_?

_____

_____

_____

_____

_____

_____

"Weekly **reviews** help you reflect on your previous week. Weekly **previews** set you up for next week's success."

WEEKLY PREVIEW

VISION / Review your *vision* to help you remember what you want to accomplish in your six life domains.

QUARTERLY GOAL REVIEW / Write down the goals that you are focused on this quarter.

Goal 1: _____
_____
_____

    Next Action Steps:

    _____
    _____
    _____
    _____

Goal 2: _____
_____
_____

    Next Action Steps:

    _____
    _____
    _____
    _____

Goal 3: _____
_____
_____

    Next Action Steps:

    _____
    _____
    _____
    _____

WEEKLY PREVIEW

3 WEEKLY THRIVE ACTIONS / Write out the most important steps to help you move closer to your goals this week.

Action 1: _____

_____

_____

Action 2: _____

_____

_____

Action 3: _____

_____

_____

THIS WEEK AT A GLANCE / Write out any other personal or professional tasks that you have for this week.

PERSONAL

_____

_____

_____

_____

_____

_____

_____

PROFESSIONAL

_____

_____

_____

_____

_____

_____

_____

MONDAY

AGENDA | SCHEDULE

3 DAILY THRIVE ACTIONS
List the top 3 *to-do's* to get you closer to your goals.

_____

◯ _____
   _____

◯ _____
   _____

◯ _____
   _____

_____

DAILY TASKS

DAILY TRIUMPHS

6 _____
  _____
7 _____
  _____
8 _____
  _____
9 _____
  _____
10 _____
  _____
11 _____
  _____
12 _____
  _____
1 _____
  _____
2 _____
  _____
3 _____
  _____
4 _____
  _____
5 _____
  _____
6 _____
  _____
7 _____
  _____
8 _____
  _____

DAILY NOTES

TUESDAY

AGENDA | SCHEDULE

3 DAILY THRIVE ACTIONS
List the top 3 *to-do's* to get you closer to your goals.

○ _____

○ _____

○ _____

DAILY TASKS

DAILY TRIUMPHS

6

7

8

9

10

11

12

1

2

3

4

5

6

7

8

DAILY NOTES

WEDNESDAY

3 DAILY THRIVE ACTIONS

List the top 3 *to-do's* to get you closer to your goals.

○ _____

○ _____

○ _____

6 _____

7 _____

8 _____

9 _____

10 _____

11 _____

12 _____

DAILY TASKS

1 _____

2 _____

3 _____

4 _____

DAILY TRIUMPHS

5 _____

6 _____

7 _____

8 _____

DAILY NOTES

THURSDAY

AGENDA | SCHEDULE

3 DAILY THRIVE ACTIONS
List the top 3 *to-do's* to get you closer to your goals.

◯ _____

◯ _____

◯ _____

DAILY TASKS

DAILY TRIUMPHS

6 _____

7 _____

8 _____

9 _____

10 _____

11 _____

12 _____

1 _____

2 _____

3 _____

4 _____

5 _____

6 _____

7 _____

8 _____

DAILY NOTES

FRIDAY

AGENDA | SCHEDULE

3 DAILY THRIVE ACTIONS
List the top 3 *to-do's* to get you closer to your goals.

◯ _____

◯ _____

◯ _____

DAILY TASKS

DAILY TRIUMPHS

6 ——————————

7 ——————————

8 ——————————

9 ——————————

10 ——————————

11 ——————————

12 ——————————

1 ——————————

2 ——————————

3 ——————————

4 ——————————

5 ——————————

6 ——————————

7 ——————————

8 ——————————

DAILY NOTES

SATURDAY

AGENDA | SCHEDULE

3 DAILY THRIVE ACTIONS
List the top 3 *to-do's* to get you closer to your goals.

○ _____

○ _____

○ _____

DAILY TASKS

DAILY TRIUMPHS

6 _____

7 _____

8 _____

9 _____

10 _____

11 _____

12 _____

1 _____

2 _____

3 _____

4 _____

5 _____

6 _____

7 _____

8 _____

DAILY NOTES

SUNDAY

3 DAILY THRIVE ACTIONS
List the top 3 *to-do's* to get you closer to your goals.

○ _____

○ _____

○ _____

DAILY TASKS

DAILY TRIUMPHS

6 _____

7 _____

8 _____

9 _____

10 _____

11 _____

12 _____

1 _____

2 _____

3 _____

4 _____

5 _____

6 _____

7 _____

8 _____

DAILY NOTES

WEEKLY REVIEW

STEP 1. BIGGEST TRIUMPHS / List your top accomplishments from the last week.

_____

_____

_____

_____

_____

_____

STEP 2. HOW FAR DID YOU GET ON YOUR 3 WEEKLY THRIVE ACTIONS?

_____

_____

_____

_____

_____

_____

STEP 3. WHAT WORKED AND WHAT DIDN'T?

_____

_____

_____

_____

_____

_____

STEP 4. MISSION STATEMENT REVIEW / Refer back to your *mission*. How well did you live out your *mission* this past week? What do you need to do this week to better live out your *mission*?

_____

_____

_____

_____

_____

_____

"Weekly **reviews** help you reflect on your previous week. Weekly **previews** set you up for next week's success."

WEEKLY PREVIEW

VISION / Review your *vision* to help you remember what you want to accomplish in your six life domains.

QUARTERLY GOAL REVIEW / Write down the goals that you are focused on this quarter.

Goal 1: _____

_____

_____

    Next Action Steps:

    _____

    _____

    _____

    _____

Goal 2: _____

_____

    Next Action Steps:

    _____

    _____

    _____

    _____

Goal 3: _____

_____

    Next Action Steps:

    _____

    _____

    _____

    _____

WEEKLY PREVIEW

3 WEEKLY THRIVE ACTIONS / Write out the most important steps to help you move closer to your goals this week.

Action 1: _____

_____

_____

Action 2: _____

_____

_____

Action 3: _____

_____

_____

THIS WEEK AT A GLANCE/ Write out any other personal or professional tasks that you have for this week.

PERSONAL

_____

_____

_____

_____

_____

_____

_____

PROFESSIONAL

_____

_____

_____

_____

_____

_____

_____

MONDAY

AGENDA | SCHEDULE

3 DAILY THRIVE ACTIONS
List the top 3 *to-do's* to get you closer to your goals.

_____

◯ _____
   _____

◯ _____
   _____

◯ _____
   _____

_____

DAILY TASKS

DAILY TRIUMPHS

6 _____

7 _____

8 _____

9 _____

10 _____

11 _____

12 _____

1 _____

2 _____

3 _____

4 _____

5 _____

6 _____

7 _____

8 _____

DAILY NOTES

TUESDAY

AGENDA | SCHEDULE

3 DAILY THRIVE ACTIONS

List the top 3 *to-do's* to get you closer to your goals.

○ _____

○ _____

○ _____

DAILY TASKS

DAILY TRIUMPHS

6 _____

7 _____

8 _____

9 _____

10 _____

11 _____

12 _____

1 _____

2 _____

3 _____

4 _____

5 _____

6 _____

7 _____

8 _____

DAILY NOTES

WEDNESDAY

AGENDA | SCHEDULE

3 DAILY THRIVE ACTIONS

List the top 3 *to-do's* to get you closer to your goals.

◯ _____

◯ _____

◯ _____

6 _____

7 _____

8 _____

9 _____

10 _____

11 _____

12 _____

DAILY TASKS

1 _____

2 _____

3 _____

4 _____

DAILY TRIUMPHS

5 _____

6 _____

7 _____

8 _____

DAILY NOTES

THURSDAY

AGENDA | SCHEDULE

3 DAILY THRIVE ACTIONS
List the top 3 *to-do's* to get you closer to your goals.

○ _____

○ _____

○ _____

DAILY TASKS

DAILY TRIUMPHS

6 _____

7 _____

8 _____

9 _____

10 _____

11 _____

12 _____

1 _____

2 _____

3 _____

4 _____

5 _____

6 _____

7 _____

8 _____

DAILY NOTES

FRIDAY

AGENDA | SCHEDULE

3 DAILY THRIVE ACTIONS
List the top 3 *to-do's* to get you closer to your goals.

◯ _____

◯ _____

◯ _____

DAILY TASKS

DAILY TRIUMPHS

6 _____

7 _____

8 _____

9 _____

10 _____

11 _____

12 _____

1 _____

2 _____

3 _____

4 _____

5 _____

6 _____

7 _____

8 _____

DAILY NOTES

SATURDAY

AGENDA | SCHEDULE

3 DAILY THRIVE ACTIONS
List the top 3 *to-do's* to get you closer to your goals.

○ _____

○ _____

○ _____

DAILY TASKS

DAILY TRIUMPHS

6 _____

7 _____

8 _____

9 _____

10 _____

11 _____

12 _____

1 _____

2 _____

3 _____

4 _____

5 _____

6 _____

7 _____

8 _____

DAILY NOTES

SUNDAY

AGENDA | SCHEDULE

3 DAILY THRIVE ACTIONS
List the top 3 *to-do's* to get you closer to your goals.

◯ _____

◯ _____

◯ _____

_____

DAILY TASKS

DAILY TRIUMPHS

6 _____

7 _____

8 _____

9 _____

10 _____

11 _____

12 _____

1 _____

2 _____

3 _____

4 _____

5 _____

6 _____

7 _____

8 _____

DAILY NOTES

WEEKLY REVIEW

STEP 1. BIGGEST TRIUMPHS / List your top accomplishments from the last week.

_____

_____

_____

_____

_____

_____

STEP 2. HOW FAR DID YOU GET ON YOUR 3 WEEKLY THRIVE ACTIONS?

_____

_____

_____

_____

_____

_____

STEP 3. WHAT WORKED AND WHAT DIDN'T?

_____

_____

_____

_____

_____

_____

STEP 4. MISSION STATEMENT REVIEW / Refer back to your *mission*. How well did you live out your *mission* this past week? What do you need to do this week to better live out your *mission*?

_____

_____

_____

_____

_____

_____

"Weekly **reviews** help you reflect on your previous week. Weekly **previews** set you up for next week's success."

WEEKLY PREVIEW

VISION / Review your *vision* to help you remember what you want to accomplish in your six life domains.

QUARTERLY GOAL REVIEW / Write down the goals that you are focused on this quarter.

Goal 1: _____

_____

_____

    Next Action Steps:

    _____

    _____

    _____

    _____

Goal 2: _____

_____

_____

    Next Action Steps:

    _____

    _____

    _____

    _____

Goal 3: _____

_____

_____

    Next Action Steps:

    _____

    _____

    _____

    _____

WEEKLY PREVIEW

3 WEEKLY THRIVE ACTIONS / Write out the most important steps to help you move closer to your goals this week.

Action 1: _____

_____

_____

Action 2: _____

_____

_____

Action 3: _____

_____

_____

THIS WEEK AT A GLANCE / Write out any other personal or professional tasks that you have for this week.

PERSONAL

_____

_____

_____

_____

_____

_____

_____

PROFESSIONAL

_____

_____

_____

_____

_____

_____

_____

MONDAY

AGENDA | SCHEDULE

3 DAILY THRIVE ACTIONS
List the top 3 *to-do's* to get you closer to your goals.

○ _____

○ _____

○ _____

DAILY TASKS

DAILY TRIUMPHS

6 _____

7 _____

8 _____

9 _____

10 _____

11 _____

12 _____

1 _____

2 _____

3 _____

4 _____

5 _____

6 _____

7 _____

8 _____

DAILY NOTES

TUESDAY

AGENDA | SCHEDULE

3 DAILY THRIVE ACTIONS
List the top 3 *to-do's* to get you closer to your goals.

○ _____

○ _____

○ _____

DAILY TASKS

DAILY TRIUMPHS

6 _____

7 _____

8 _____

9 _____

10 _____

11 _____

12 _____

1 _____

2 _____

3 _____

4 _____

5 _____

6 _____

7 _____

8 _____

DAILY NOTES

WEDNESDAY

AGENDA | SCHEDULE

3 DAILY THRIVE ACTIONS
List the top 3 *to-do's* to get you closer to your goals.

○ _____

○ _____

○ _____

DAILY TASKS

DAILY TRIUMPHS

6 _____

7 _____

8 _____

9 _____

10 _____

11 _____

12 _____

1 _____

2 _____

3 _____

4 _____

5 _____

6 _____

7 _____

8 _____

DAILY NOTES

THURSDAY

AGENDA | SCHEDULE

3 DAILY THRIVE ACTIONS

List the top 3 *to-do's* to get you closer to your goals.

○ _____

○ _____

○ _____

DAILY TASKS

DAILY TRIUMPHS

6 _____

7 _____

8 _____

9 _____

10 _____

11 _____

12 _____

1 _____

2 _____

3 _____

4 _____

5 _____

6 _____

7 _____

8 _____

DAILY NOTES

FRIDAY

AGENDA | SCHEDULE

3 DAILY THRIVE ACTIONS

List the top 3 *to-do's* to get you closer to your goals.

◯ _____

◯ _____

◯ _____

6 _____

7 _____

8 _____

9 _____

10 _____

11 _____

12 _____

DAILY TASKS

1 _____

2 _____

3 _____

4 _____

DAILY TRIUMPHS

5 _____

6 _____

7 _____

8 _____

DAILY NOTES

SATURDAY

AGENDA | SCHEDULE

3 DAILY THRIVE ACTIONS

List the top 3 *to-do's* to get you closer to your goals.

○ _____

○ _____

○ _____

DAILY TASKS

DAILY TRIUMPHS

6 _____

7 _____

8 _____

9 _____

10 _____

11 _____

12 _____

1 _____

2 _____

3 _____

4 _____

5 _____

6 _____

7 _____

8 _____

DAILY NOTES

SUNDAY

AGENDA | SCHEDULE

3 DAILY THRIVE ACTIONS

List the top 3 *to-do's* to get you closer to your goals.

○ _____

○ _____

○ _____

DAILY TASKS

DAILY TRIUMPHS

6 _____

7 _____

8 _____

9 _____

10 _____

11 _____

12 _____

1 _____

2 _____

3 _____

4 _____

5 _____

6 _____

7 _____

8 _____

110

DAILY NOTES

WEEKLY REVIEW

STEP 1. BIGGEST TRIUMPHS / List your top accomplishments from the last week.

_____

_____

_____

_____

_____

_____

STEP 2. HOW FAR DID YOU GET ON YOUR 3 WEEKLY THRIVE ACTIONS?

_____

_____

_____

_____

_____

_____

STEP 3. WHAT WORKED AND WHAT DIDN'T?

_____

_____

_____

_____

_____

_____

STEP 4. MISSION STATEMENT REVIEW / Refer back to your *mission*. How well did you live out your *mission* this past week? What do you need to do this week to better live out your *mission*?

_____

_____

_____

_____

_____

"Weekly **reviews** help you reflect on
your previous week. Weekly **previews**
set you up for next week's success."

WEEKLY PREVIEW

VISION / Review your *vision* to help you remember what you want to accomplish in your six life domains.

QUARTERLY GOAL REVIEW / Write down the goals that you are focused on this quarter.

Goal 1: _____

_____

_____

    Next Action Steps:

    _____

    _____

    _____

    _____

Goal 2: _____

_____

_____

    Next Action Steps:

    _____

    _____

    _____

    _____

Goal 3: _____

_____

_____

    Next Action Steps:

    _____

    _____

    _____

    _____

WEEKLY PREVIEW

3 WEEKLY THRIVE ACTIONS / Write out the most important steps to help you move closer to your goals this week.

Action 1: _____

_____

_____

Action 2: _____

_____

_____

Action 3: _____

_____

_____

THIS WEEK AT A GLANCE / Write out any other personal or professional tasks that you have for this week.

PERSONAL

_____

_____

_____

_____

_____

_____

PROFESSIONAL

_____

_____

_____

_____

_____

_____

MONDAY

3 DAILY THRIVE ACTIONS

List the top 3 *to-do's* to get you closer to your goals.

◯ _____

◯ _____

◯ _____

DAILY TASKS

DAILY TRIUMPHS

6 _____

7 _____

8 _____

9 _____

10 _____

11 _____

12 _____

1 _____

2 _____

3 _____

4 _____

5 _____

6 _____

7 _____

8 _____

DAILY NOTES

TUESDAY

AGENDA | SCHEDULE

3 DAILY THRIVE ACTIONS

List the top 3 *to-do's* to get you closer to your goals.

○ _____

○ _____

○ _____

DAILY TASKS

DAILY TRIUMPHS

6 _____

7 _____

8 _____

9 _____

10 _____

11 _____

12 _____

1 _____

2 _____

3 _____

4 _____

5 _____

6 _____

7 _____

8 _____

DAILY NOTES

WEDNESDAY

AGENDA | SCHEDULE

3 DAILY THRIVE ACTIONS

List the top 3 *to-do's* to get you closer to your goals.

6 _____

7 _____

8 _____

9 _____

10 _____

11 _____

12 _____

DAILY TASKS

1 _____

2 _____

3 _____

4 _____

DAILY TRIUMPHS

5 _____

6 _____

7 _____

8 _____

DAILY NOTES

THURSDAY

AGENDA | SCHEDULE

3 DAILY THRIVE ACTIONS

List the top 3 *to-do's* to get you closer to your goals.

○ _____

○ _____

○ _____

DAILY TASKS

DAILY TRIUMPHS

6 _____

7 _____

8 _____

9 _____

10 _____

11 _____

12 _____

1 _____

2 _____

3 _____

4 _____

5 _____

6 _____

7 _____

8 _____

DAILY NOTES

FRIDAY

AGENDA | SCHEDULE

3 DAILY THRIVE ACTIONS

List the top 3 *to-do's* to get you closer to your goals.

○ _____

○ _____

○ _____

DAILY TASKS

DAILY TRIUMPHS

6 _____

7 _____

8 _____

9 _____

10 _____

11 _____

12 _____

1 _____

2 _____

3 _____

4 _____

5 _____

6 _____

7 _____

8 _____

DAILY NOTES

SATURDAY

AGENDA | SCHEDULE

3 DAILY THRIVE ACTIONS
List the top 3 *to-do's* to get you closer to your goals.

○ _____

○ _____

○ _____

DAILY TASKS

DAILY TRIUMPHS

6 _____

7 _____

8 _____

9 _____

10 _____

11 _____

12 _____

1 _____

2 _____

3 _____

4 _____

5 _____

6 _____

7 _____

8 _____

DAILY NOTES

SUNDAY

AGENDA | SCHEDULE

3 DAILY THRIVE ACTIONS
List the top 3 *to-do's* to get you closer to your goals.

◯ _____

◯ _____

◯ _____

DAILY TASKS

DAILY TRIUMPHS

6 _____

7 _____

8 _____

9 _____

10 _____

11 _____

12 _____

1 _____

2 _____

3 _____

4 _____

5 _____

6 _____

7 _____

8 _____

DAILY NOTES

WEEKLY REVIEW

STEP 1. BIGGEST TRIUMPHS / List your top accomplishments from the last week.

_____

_____

_____

_____

_____

_____

STEP 2. HOW FAR DID YOU GET ON YOUR 3 WEEKLY THRIVE ACTIONS?

_____

_____

_____

_____

_____

_____

STEP 3. WHAT WORKED AND WHAT DIDN'T?

_____

_____

_____

_____

_____

_____

STEP 4. MISSION STATEMENT REVIEW / Refer back to your *mission*. How well did you live out your *mission* this past week? What do you need to do this week to better live out your *mission*?

_____

_____

_____

_____

_____

_____

"Weekly **reviews** help you reflect on your previous week. Weekly **previews** set you up for next week's success."

WEEKLY PREVIEW

VISION / Review your *vision* to help you remember what you want to accomplish in your six life domains.

QUARTERLY GOAL REVIEW / Write down the goals that you are focused on this quarter.

Goal 1: _____

_____

_____

    Next Action Steps:

    _____

    _____

    _____

    _____

Goal 2: _____

_____

_____

    Next Action Steps:

    _____

    _____

    _____

    _____

Goal 3: _____

_____

_____

    Next Action Steps:

    _____

    _____

    _____

    _____

WEEKLY PREVIEW

3 WEEKLY THRIVE ACTIONS / Write out the most important steps to help you move closer to your goals this week.

Action 1: _____
_____
_____

Action 2: _____
_____
_____

Action 3: _____
_____
_____

THIS WEEK AT A GLANCE / Write out any other personal or professional tasks that you have for this week.

PERSONAL

_____
_____
_____
_____
_____
_____
_____

PROFESSIONAL

_____
_____
_____
_____
_____
_____
_____

MONDAY

AGENDA | SCHEDULE

3 DAILY THRIVE ACTIONS

List the top 3 *to-do's* to get you closer to your goals.

○ _____

○ _____

○ _____

6 _____

7 _____

8 _____

9 _____

10 _____

11 _____

12 _____

DAILY TASKS

1 _____

2 _____

3 _____

4 _____

DAILY TRIUMPHS

5 _____

6 _____

7 _____

8 _____

DAILY NOTES

TUESDAY

AGENDA | SCHEDULE

3 DAILY THRIVE ACTIONS

List the top 3 *to-do's* to get you closer to your goals.

○ _____

○ _____

○ _____

DAILY TASKS

DAILY TRIUMPHS

6 _____

7 _____

8 _____

9 _____

10 _____

11 _____

12 _____

1 _____

2 _____

3 _____

4 _____

5 _____

6 _____

7 _____

8 _____

DAILY NOTES

WEDNESDAY

AGENDA | SCHEDULE

3 DAILY THRIVE ACTIONS

List the top 3 *to-do's* to get you closer to your goals.

○ _____

○ _____

○ _____

DAILY TASKS

DAILY TRIUMPHS

6 _____

7 _____

8 _____

9 _____

10 _____

11 _____

12 _____

1 _____

2 _____

3 _____

4 _____

5 _____

6 _____

7 _____

8 _____

DAILY NOTES

THURSDAY

AGENDA | SCHEDULE

3 DAILY THRIVE ACTIONS

List the top 3 *to-do's* to get you closer to your goals.

○ _____

○ _____

○ _____

DAILY TASKS

DAILY TRIUMPHS

6 _____

7 _____

8 _____

9 _____

10 _____

11 _____

12 _____

1 _____

2 _____

3 _____

4 _____

5 _____

6 _____

7 _____

8 _____

DAILY NOTES

FRIDAY

3 DAILY THRIVE ACTIONS
List the top 3 *to-do's* to get you closer to your goals.

○

○

○

DAILY TASKS

DAILY TRIUMPHS

6

7

8

9

10

11

12

1

2

3

4

5

6

7

8

DAILY NOTES

SATURDAY

AGENDA | SCHEDULE

3 DAILY THRIVE ACTIONS
List the top 3 *to-do's* to get you closer to your goals.

○ _____

○ _____

○ _____

DAILY TASKS

DAILY TRIUMPHS

6 _____

7 _____

8 _____

9 _____

10 _____

11 _____

12 _____

1 _____

2 _____

3 _____

4 _____

5 _____

6 _____

7 _____

8 _____

DAILY NOTES

SUNDAY

AGENDA | SCHEDULE

3 DAILY THRIVE ACTIONS
List the top 3 *to-do's* to get you closer to your goals.

○ _____

○ _____

○ _____

DAILY TASKS

DAILY TRIUMPHS

6 _____

7 _____

8 _____

9 _____

10 _____

11 _____

12 _____

1 _____

2 _____

3 _____

4 _____

5 _____

6 _____

7 _____

8 _____

DAILY NOTES

WEEKLY REVIEW

STEP 1. BIGGEST TRIUMPHS / List your top accomplishments from the last week.

_____

_____

_____

_____

_____

_____

STEP 2. HOW FAR DID YOU GET ON YOUR 3 WEEKLY THRIVE ACTIONS?

_____

_____

_____

_____

_____

STEP 3. WHAT WORKED AND WHAT DIDN'T?

_____

_____

_____

_____

_____

_____

STEP 4. MISSION STATEMENT REVIEW / Refer back to your *mission*. How well did you live out your *mission* this past week? What do you need to do this week to better live out your *mission*?

_____

_____

_____

_____

_____

_____

"Weekly **reviews** help you reflect on
your previous week. Weekly **previews**
set you up for next week's success."

WEEKLY PREVIEW

VISION / Review your *vision* to help you remember what you want to accomplish in your six life domains.

QUARTERLY GOAL REVIEW / Write down the goals that you are focused on this quarter.

Goal 1: _____

_____

_____

Next Action Steps:

_____

_____

_____

_____

Goal 2: _____

_____

_____

Next Action Steps:

_____

_____

_____

_____

Goal 3: _____

_____

_____

Next Action Steps:

_____

_____

_____

_____

WEEKLY PREVIEW

3 WEEKLY THRIVE ACTIONS / Write out the most important steps to help you move closer to your goals this week.

Action 1: _____

_____

_____

Action 2: _____

_____

_____

Action 3: _____

_____

_____

THIS WEEK AT A GLANCE / Write out any other personal or professional tasks that you have for this week.

PERSONAL

_____

_____

_____

_____

_____

_____

_____

PROFESSIONAL

_____

_____

_____

_____

_____

_____

_____

MONDAY

AGENDA | SCHEDULE

3 DAILY THRIVE ACTIONS

List the top 3 *to-do's* to get you closer to your goals.

◯ _____

◯ _____

◯ _____

DAILY TASKS

DAILY TRIUMPHS

6 _____

7 _____

8 _____

9 _____

10 _____

11 _____

12 _____

1 _____

2 _____

3 _____

4 _____

5 _____

6 _____

7 _____

8 _____

DAILY NOTES

TUESDAY

AGENDA | SCHEDULE

3 DAILY THRIVE ACTIONS
List the top 3 *to-do's* to get you closer to your goals.

○ _____

○ _____

○ _____

DAILY TASKS

DAILY TRIUMPHS

6 _____

7 _____

8 _____

9 _____

10 _____

11 _____

12 _____

1 _____

2 _____

3 _____

4 _____

5 _____

6 _____

7 _____

8 _____

DAILY NOTES

WEDNESDAY

AGENDA | SCHEDULE

3 DAILY THRIVE ACTIONS
List the top 3 *to-do's* to get you closer to your goals.

○ _____

○ _____

○ _____

DAILY TASKS

DAILY TRIUMPHS

6 _____

7 _____

8 _____

9 _____

10 _____

11 _____

12 _____

1 _____

2 _____

3 _____

4 _____

5 _____

6 _____

7 _____

8 _____

DAILY NOTES

THURSDAY

3 DAILY THRIVE ACTIONS

List the top 3 *to-do's* to get you closer to your goals.

○ _____

○ _____

○ _____

DAILY TASKS

DAILY TRIUMPHS

AGENDA | SCHEDULE

6

7

8

9

10

11

12

1

2

3

4

5

6

7

8

DAILY NOTES

FRIDAY

AGENDA | SCHEDULE

3 DAILY THRIVE ACTIONS
List the top 3 *to-do's* to get you closer to your goals.

○ _____

○ _____

○ _____

DAILY TASKS

DAILY TRIUMPHS

6 _____

7 _____

8 _____

9 _____

10 _____

11 _____

12 _____

1 _____

2 _____

3 _____

4 _____

5 _____

6 _____

7 _____

8 _____

DAILY NOTES

SATURDAY

AGENDA | SCHEDULE

3 DAILY THRIVE ACTIONS

List the top 3 *to-do's* to get you closer to your goals.

○ _____

○ _____

○ _____

DAILY TASKS

DAILY TRIUMPHS

6 _____

7 _____

8 _____

9 _____

10 _____

11 _____

12 _____

1 _____

2 _____

3 _____

4 _____

5 _____

6 _____

7 _____

8 _____

DAILY NOTES

SUNDAY

AGENDA | SCHEDULE

3 DAILY THRIVE ACTIONS
List the top 3 *to-do's* to get you closer to your goals.

○ _____

○ _____

○ _____

DAILY TASKS

DAILY TRIUMPHS

6 _____

7 _____

8 _____

9 _____

10 _____

11 _____

12 _____

1 _____

2 _____

3 _____

4 _____

5 _____

6 _____

7 _____

8 _____

DAILY NOTES

WEEKLY REVIEW

STEP 1. BIGGEST TRIUMPHS / List your top accomplishments from the last week.

_____

_____

_____

_____

_____

_____

STEP 2. HOW FAR DID YOU GET ON YOUR 3 WEEKLY THRIVE ACTIONS?

_____

_____

_____

_____

_____

_____

STEP 3. WHAT WORKED AND WHAT DIDN'T?

_____

_____

_____

_____

_____

_____

STEP 4. MISSION STATEMENT REVIEW / Refer back to your *mission*. How well did you live out your *mission* this past week? What do you need to do this week to better live out your *mission*?

_____

_____

_____

_____

_____

_____

"Weekly **reviews** help you reflect on your previous week. Weekly **previews** set you up for next week's success."

WEEKLY PREVIEW

VISION / Review your *vision* to help you remember what you want to accomplish in your six life domains.

QUARTERLY GOAL REVIEW / Write down the goals that you are focused on this quarter.

Goal 1: _____

_____

_____

   Next Action Steps:

   _____

   _____

   _____

   _____

Goal 2: _____

_____

_____

   Next Action Steps:

   _____

   _____

   _____

   _____

Goal 3: _____

_____

_____

   Next Action Steps:

   _____

   _____

   _____

   _____

WEEKLY PREVIEW

3 WEEKLY THRIVE ACTIONS / Write out the most important steps to help you move closer to your goals this week.

Action 1: _____

_____

_____

Action 2: _____

_____

_____

Action 3: _____

_____

_____

THIS WEEK AT A GLANCE / Write out any other personal or professional tasks that you have for this week.

PERSONAL

_____

_____

_____

_____

_____

_____

_____

PROFESSIONAL

_____

_____

_____

_____

_____

_____

_____

MONDAY

AGENDA | SCHEDULE

3 DAILY THRIVE ACTIONS

List the top 3 *to-do's* to get you closer to your goals.

○ _____

○ _____

○ _____

DAILY TASKS

DAILY TRIUMPHS

6 _____

7 _____

8 _____

9 _____

10 _____

11 _____

12 _____

1 _____

2 _____

3 _____

4 _____

5 _____

6 _____

7 _____

8 _____

DAILY NOTES

TUESDAY

AGENDA | SCHEDULE

3 DAILY THRIVE ACTIONS

List the top 3 *to-do's* to get you closer to your goals.

O _____

O _____

O _____

DAILY TASKS

DAILY TRIUMPHS

6 _____

7 _____

8 _____

9 _____

10 _____

11 _____

12 _____

1 _____

2 _____

3 _____

4 _____

5 _____

6 _____

7 _____

8 _____

DAILY NOTES

WEDNESDAY

AGENDA | SCHEDULE

3 DAILY THRIVE ACTIONS
List the top 3 *to-do's* to get you closer to your goals.

O _____

O _____

O _____

DAILY TASKS

DAILY TRIUMPHS

6 _____

7 _____

8 _____

9 _____

10 _____

11 _____

12 _____

1 _____

2 _____

3 _____

4 _____

5 _____

6 _____

7 _____

8 _____

DAILY NOTES

THURSDAY

3 DAILY THRIVE ACTIONS

List the top 3 *to-do's* to get you closer to your goals.

○ _____

○ _____

○ _____

DAILY TASKS

DAILY TRIUMPHS

6 _____

7 _____

8 _____

9 _____

10 _____

11 _____

12 _____

1 _____

2 _____

3 _____

4 _____

5 _____

6 _____

7 _____

8 _____

DAILY NOTES

FRIDAY

3 DAILY THRIVE ACTIONS

List the top 3 *to-do's* to get you closer to your goals.

○ _____

○ _____

○ _____

DAILY TASKS

DAILY TRIUMPHS

6 _____

7 _____

8 _____

9 _____

10 _____

11 _____

12 _____

1 _____

2 _____

3 _____

4 _____

5 _____

6 _____

7 _____

8 _____

DAILY NOTES

SATURDAY

AGENDA | SCHEDULE

3 DAILY THRIVE ACTIONS
List the top 3 *to-do's* to get you closer to your goals.

○ _____

○ _____

○ _____

DAILY TASKS

DAILY TRIUMPHS

6 _____

7 _____

8 _____

9 _____

10 _____

11 _____

12 _____

1 _____

2 _____

3 _____

4 _____

5 _____

6 _____

7 _____

8 _____

DAILY NOTES

SUNDAY

AGENDA | SCHEDULE

3 DAILY THRIVE ACTIONS

List the top 3 *to-do's* to get you closer to your goals.

○ _____

○ _____

○ _____

DAILY TASKS

DAILY TRIUMPHS

6 _____

7 _____

8 _____

9 _____

10 _____

11 _____

12 _____

1 _____

2 _____

3 _____

4 _____

5 _____

6 _____

7 _____

8 _____

DAILY NOTES

WEEKLY REVIEW

STEP 1. BIGGEST TRIUMPHS / List your top accomplishments from the last week.

_____

_____

_____

_____

_____

_____

STEP 2. HOW FAR DID YOU GET ON YOUR 3 WEEKLY THRIVE ACTIONS?

_____

_____

_____

_____

_____

STEP 3. WHAT WORKED AND WHAT DIDN'T?

_____

_____

_____

_____

_____

STEP 4. MISSION STATEMENT REVIEW / Refer back to your *mission*. How well did you live out your *mission* this past week? What do you need to do this week to better live out your *mission*?

_____

_____

_____

_____

_____

"Weekly **reviews** help you reflect on your previous week. Weekly **previews** set you up for next week's success."

WEEKLY PREVIEW

VISION / Review your *vision* to help you remember what you want to accomplish in your six life domains.

QUARTERLY GOAL REVIEW / Write down the goals that you are focused on this quarter.

Goal 1: _____

_____

_____

    Next Action Steps:

    _____

    _____

    _____

    _____

Goal 2: _____

_____

_____

    Next Action Steps:

    _____

    _____

    _____

    _____

Goal 3: _____

_____

_____

    Next Action Steps:

    _____

    _____

    _____

    _____

WEEKLY PREVIEW

3 WEEKLY THRIVE ACTIONS / Write out the most important steps to help you move closer to your goals this week.

Action 1: _____

_____

_____

Action 2: _____

_____

_____

Action 3: _____

_____

_____

THIS WEEK AT A GLANCE / Write out any other personal or professional tasks that you have for this week.

PERSONAL

_____

_____

_____

_____

_____

_____

_____

PROFESSIONAL

_____

_____

_____

_____

_____

_____

_____

MONDAY

AGENDA | SCHEDULE

3 DAILY THRIVE ACTIONS
List the top 3 *to-do's* to get you closer to your goals.

○ _____

○ _____

○ _____

DAILY TASKS

DAILY TRIUMPHS

6 _____

7 _____

8 _____

9 _____

10 _____

11 _____

12 _____

1 _____

2 _____

3 _____

4 _____

5 _____

6 _____

7 _____

8 _____

DAILY NOTES

TUESDAY

AGENDA | SCHEDULE

3 DAILY THRIVE ACTIONS
List the top 3 *to-do's* to get you closer to your goals.

○ _____

○ _____

○ _____

DAILY TASKS

DAILY TRIUMPHS

6 _____

7 _____

8 _____

9 _____

10 _____

11 _____

12 _____

1 _____

2 _____

3 _____

4 _____

5 _____

6 _____

7 _____

8 _____

DAILY NOTES

WEDNESDAY

AGENDA | SCHEDULE

3 DAILY THRIVE ACTIONS
List the top 3 *to-do's* to get you closer to your goals.

○ _____

○ _____

○ _____

DAILY TASKS

DAILY TRIUMPHS

6 _____

7 _____

8 _____

9 _____

10 _____

11 _____

12 _____

1 _____

2 _____

3 _____

4 _____

5 _____

6 _____

7 _____

8 _____

DAILY NOTES

THURSDAY

AGENDA | SCHEDULE

3 DAILY THRIVE ACTIONS

List the top 3 *to-do's* to get you closer to your goals.

○ _____

○ _____

○ _____

DAILY TASKS

DAILY TRIUMPHS

6 _____

7 _____

8 _____

9 _____

10 _____

11 _____

12 _____

1 _____

2 _____

3 _____

4 _____

5 _____

6 _____

7 _____

8 _____

DAILY NOTES

FRIDAY

AGENDA | SCHEDULE

3 DAILY THRIVE ACTIONS
List the top 3 *to-do's* to get you closer to your goals.

○ _____

○ _____

○ _____

DAILY TASKS

DAILY TRIUMPHS

6 _____

7 _____

8 _____

9 _____

10 _____

11 _____

12 _____

1 _____

2 _____

3 _____

4 _____

5 _____

6 _____

7 _____

8 _____

DAILY NOTES

SATURDAY

AGENDA | SCHEDULE

3 DAILY THRIVE ACTIONS
List the top 3 *to-do's* to get you closer to your goals.

◯ _____

◯ _____

◯ _____

DAILY TASKS

DAILY TRIUMPHS

6 _____

7 _____

8 _____

9 _____

10 _____

11 _____

12 _____

1 _____

2 _____

3 _____

4 _____

5 _____

6 _____

7 _____

8 _____

DAILY NOTES

SUNDAY

AGENDA | SCHEDULE

3 DAILY THRIVE ACTIONS
List the top 3 *to-do's* to get you closer to your goals.

○ _____

○ _____

○ _____

DAILY TASKS

DAILY TRIUMPHS

6 _____

7 _____

8 _____

9 _____

10 _____

11 _____

12 _____

1 _____

2 _____

3 _____

4 _____

5 _____

6 _____

7 _____

8 _____

DAILY NOTES

WEEKLY REVIEW

STEP 1. BIGGEST TRIUMPHS / List your top accomplishments from the last week.

_____

_____

_____

_____

_____

_____

STEP 2. HOW FAR DID YOU GET ON YOUR 3 WEEKLY THRIVE ACTIONS?

_____

_____

_____

_____

_____

STEP 3. WHAT WORKED AND WHAT DIDN'T?

_____

_____

_____

_____

_____

STEP 4. MISSION STATEMENT REVIEW / Refer back to your _mission_. How well did you live out your _mission_ this past week? What do you need to do this week to better live out your _mission_?

_____

_____

_____

_____

_____

"Weekly **reviews** help you reflect on your previous week. Weekly **previews** set you up for next week's success."

WEEKLY PREVIEW

VISION / Review your *vision* to help you remember what you want to accomplish in your six life domains.

QUARTERLY GOAL REVIEW / Write down the goals that you are focused on this quarter.

Goal 1: _____

_____

_____

    Next Action Steps:

    _____

    _____

    _____

    _____

Goal 2: _____

_____

_____

    Next Action Steps:

    _____

    _____

    _____

    _____

Goal 3: _____

_____

_____

    Next Action Steps:

    _____

    _____

    _____

    _____

WEEKLY PREVIEW

3 WEEKLY THRIVE ACTIONS / Write out the most important steps to help you move closer to your goals this week.

Action 1: _____

_____

_____

Action 2: _____

_____

_____

Action 3: _____

_____

_____

THIS WEEK AT A GLANCE / Write out any other personal or professional tasks that you have for this week.

PERSONAL

_____

_____

_____

_____

_____

_____

_____

PROFESSIONAL

_____

_____

_____

_____

_____

_____

_____

MONDAY

AGENDA | SCHEDULE

3 DAILY THRIVE ACTIONS
List the top 3 *to-do's* to get you closer to your goals.

◯ _____

◯ _____

◯ _____

DAILY TASKS

DAILY TRIUMPHS

6 _____

7 _____

8 _____

9 _____

10 _____

11 _____

12 _____

1 _____

2 _____

3 _____

4 _____

5 _____

6 _____

7 _____

8 _____

DAILY NOTES

TUESDAY

AGENDA | SCHEDULE

3 DAILY THRIVE ACTIONS
List the top 3 *to-do's* to get you closer to your goals.

◯

◯

◯

6 ——————————

7 ——————————

8 ——————————

9 ——————————

10 ——————————

11 ——————————

12 ——————————

DAILY TASKS

1 ——————————

2 ——————————

3 ——————————

4 ——————————

DAILY TRIUMPHS

5 ——————————

6 ——————————

7 ——————————

8 ——————————

DAILY NOTES

WEDNESDAY

AGENDA | SCHEDULE

3 DAILY THRIVE ACTIONS

List the top 3 *to-do's* to get you closer to your goals.

○ _____

○ _____

○ _____

DAILY TASKS

DAILY TRIUMPHS

6 _____

7 _____

8 _____

9 _____

10 _____

11 _____

12 _____

1 _____

2 _____

3 _____

4 _____

5 _____

6 _____

7 _____

8 _____

DAILY NOTES

THURSDAY

AGENDA | SCHEDULE

3 DAILY THRIVE ACTIONS

List the top 3 *to-do's* to get you closer to your goals.

◯ _____

◯ _____

◯ _____

DAILY TASKS

DAILY TRIUMPHS

6 —————————

7 —————————

8 —————————

9 —————————

10 —————————

11 —————————

12 —————————

1 —————————

2 —————————

3 —————————

4 —————————

5 —————————

6 —————————

7 —————————

8 —————————

DAILY NOTES

FRIDAY

AGENDA | SCHEDULE

3 DAILY THRIVE ACTIONS

List the top 3 *to-do's* to get you closer to your goals.

○ _____

○ _____

○ _____

6 _____

7 _____

8 _____

9 _____

10 _____

11 _____

12 _____

DAILY TASKS

1 _____

2 _____

3 _____

4 _____

DAILY TRIUMPHS

5 _____

6 _____

7 _____

8 _____

DAILY NOTES

SATURDAY

AGENDA | SCHEDULE

3 DAILY THRIVE ACTIONS

List the top 3 *to-do's* to get you closer to your goals.

○ _____

○ _____

○ _____

DAILY TASKS

DAILY TRIUMPHS

6 _____

7 _____

8 _____

9 _____

10 _____

11 _____

12 _____

1 _____

2 _____

3 _____

4 _____

5 _____

6 _____

7 _____

8 _____

DAILY NOTES

SUNDAY

3 DAILY THRIVE ACTIONS

List the top 3 *to-do's* to get you closer to your goals.

○ _____

○ _____

○ _____

DAILY TASKS

DAILY TRIUMPHS

6 _____

7 _____

8 _____

9 _____

10 _____

11 _____

12 _____

1 _____

2 _____

3 _____

4 _____

5 _____

6 _____

7 _____

8 _____

DAILY NOTES

WEEKLY REVIEW

STEP 1. BIGGEST TRIUMPHS / List your top accomplishments from the last week.

_____

_____

_____

_____

_____

_____

STEP 2. HOW FAR DID YOU GET ON YOUR 3 WEEKLY THRIVE ACTIONS?

_____

_____

_____

_____

_____

STEP 3. WHAT WORKED AND WHAT DIDN'T?

_____

_____

_____

_____

_____

STEP 4. MISSION STATEMENT REVIEW / Refer back to your *mission*. How well did you live out your *mission* this past week? What do you need to do this week to better live out your *mission*?

_____

_____

_____

_____

_____

"Weekly **reviews** help you reflect on your previous week. Weekly **previews** set you up for next week's success."

WEEKLY PREVIEW

VISION / Review your *vision* to help you remember what you want to accomplish in your six life domains.

QUARTERLY GOAL REVIEW / Write down the goals that you are focused on this quarter.

Goal 1: _____

_____

_____

    Next Action Steps:

    _____

    _____

    _____

    _____

Goal 2: _____

_____

_____

    Next Action Steps:

    _____

    _____

    _____

    _____

Goal 3: _____

_____

_____

    Next Action Steps:

    _____

    _____

    _____

    _____

WEEKLY PREVIEW

3 WEEKLY THRIVE ACTIONS / Write out the most important steps to help you move closer to your goals this week.

Action 1: _____
_____
_____

Action 2: _____
_____
_____

Action 3: _____
_____
_____

THIS WEEK AT A GLANCE / Write out any other personal or professional tasks that you have for this week.

PERSONAL

_____
_____
_____
_____
_____
_____
_____

PROFESSIONAL

_____
_____
_____
_____
_____
_____
_____

MONDAY

3 DAILY THRIVE ACTIONS

List the top 3 *to-do's* to get you closer to your goals.

○ _____

○ _____

○ _____

DAILY TASKS

DAILY TRIUMPHS

6 _____

7 _____

8 _____

9 _____

10 _____

11 _____

12 _____

1 _____

2 _____

3 _____

4 _____

5 _____

6 _____

7 _____

8 _____

DAILY NOTES

TUESDAY

AGENDA | SCHEDULE

3 DAILY THRIVE ACTIONS
List the top 3 *to-do's* to get you closer to your goals.

○ _____

○ _____

○ _____

DAILY TASKS

DAILY TRIUMPHS

6 _____

7 _____

8 _____

9 _____

10 _____

11 _____

12 _____

1 _____

2 _____

3 _____

4 _____

5 _____

6 _____

7 _____

8 _____

DAILY NOTES

WEDNESDAY

AGENDA | SCHEDULE

3 DAILY THRIVE ACTIONS
List the top 3 *to-do's* to get you closer to your goals.

○

○

○

DAILY TASKS

DAILY TRIUMPHS

6

7

8

9

10

11

12

1

2

3

4

5

6

7

8

DAILY NOTES

THURSDAY

3 DAILY THRIVE ACTIONS
List the top 3 *to-do's* to get you closer to your goals.

◯ _____

◯ _____

◯ _____

DAILY TASKS

DAILY TRIUMPHS

6 _____

7 _____

8 _____

9 _____

10 _____

11 _____

12 _____

1 _____

2 _____

3 _____

4 _____

5 _____

6 _____

7 _____

8 _____

DAILY NOTES

FRIDAY

AGENDA | SCHEDULE

3 DAILY THRIVE ACTIONS
List the top 3 *to-do's* to get you closer to your goals.

○ _____

○ _____

○ _____

DAILY TASKS

DAILY TRIUMPHS

6 _____

7 _____

8 _____

9 _____

10 _____

11 _____

12 _____

1 _____

2 _____

3 _____

4 _____

5 _____

6 _____

7 _____

8 _____

DAILY NOTES

SATURDAY

AGENDA | SCHEDULE

3 DAILY THRIVE ACTIONS
List the top 3 *to-do's* to get you closer to your goals.

6 _____

○ _____

7 _____

○ _____

8 _____

○ _____

9 _____

10 _____

11 _____

12 _____

DAILY TASKS

1 _____

2 _____

3 _____

4 _____

DAILY TRIUMPHS

5 _____

6 _____

7 _____

8 _____

DAILY NOTES

SUNDAY

AGENDA | SCHEDULE

3 DAILY THRIVE ACTIONS
List the top 3 *to-do's* to get you closer to your goals.

○ _____

○ _____

○ _____

DAILY TASKS

DAILY TRIUMPHS

6 _____

7 _____

8 _____

9 _____

10 _____

11 _____

12 _____

1 _____

2 _____

3 _____

4 _____

5 _____

6 _____

7 _____

8 _____

236

DAILY NOTES

WEEKLY REVIEW

STEP 1. BIGGEST TRIUMPHS / List your top accomplishments from the last week.

_____

_____

_____

_____

_____

_____

STEP 2. HOW FAR DID YOU GET ON YOUR 3 WEEKLY THRIVE ACTIONS?

_____

_____

_____

_____

_____

_____

STEP 3. WHAT WORKED AND WHAT DIDN'T?

_____

_____

_____

_____

_____

_____

STEP 4. MISSION STATEMENT REVIEW / Refer back to your *mission*. How well did you live out your *mission* this past week? What do you need to do this week to better live out your *mission*?

_____

_____

_____

_____

_____

_____

"Weekly **reviews** help you reflect on your previous week. Weekly **previews** set you up for next week's success."

WEEKLY PREVIEW

VISION / Review your *vision* to help you remember what you want to accomplish in your six life domains.

QUARTERLY GOAL REVIEW / Write down the goals that you are focused on this quarter.

Goal 1: _____

_____

_____

    Next Action Steps:

    _____

    _____

    _____

    _____

Goal 2: _____

_____

_____

    Next Action Steps:

    _____

    _____

    _____

    _____

Goal 3: _____

_____

_____

    Next Action Steps:

    _____

    _____

    _____

    _____

WEEKLY PREVIEW

3 WEEKLY THRIVE ACTIONS / Write out the most important steps to help you move closer to your goals this week.

Action 1: _____
_____
_____

Action 2: _____
_____
_____

Action 3: _____
_____
_____

THIS WEEK AT A GLANCE / Write out any other personal or professional tasks that you have for this week.

PERSONAL

_____
_____
_____
_____
_____
_____
_____

PROFESSIONAL

_____
_____
_____
_____
_____
_____
_____

MONDAY

AGENDA | SCHEDULE

3 DAILY THRIVE ACTIONS

List the top 3 *to-do's* to get you closer to your goals.

○ _____

○ _____

○ _____

DAILY TASKS

DAILY TRIUMPHS

6 _____

7 _____

8 _____

9 _____

10 _____

11 _____

12 _____

1 _____

2 _____

3 _____

4 _____

5 _____

6 _____

7 _____

8 _____

242

DAILY NOTES

TUESDAY

AGENDA | SCHEDULE

3 DAILY THRIVE ACTIONS
List the top 3 *to-do's* to get you closer to your goals.

○

○

○

DAILY TASKS

DAILY TRIUMPHS

6

7

8

9

10

11

12

1

2

3

4

5

6

7

8

DAILY NOTES

WEDNESDAY

AGENDA | SCHEDULE

3 DAILY THRIVE ACTIONS
List the top 3 *to-do's* to get you closer to your goals.

○ _____

○ _____

○ _____

DAILY TASKS

DAILY TRIUMPHS

6 _____

7 _____

8 _____

9 _____

10 _____

11 _____

12 _____

1 _____

2 _____

3 _____

4 _____

5 _____

6 _____

7 _____

8 _____

DAILY NOTES

THURSDAY

AGENDA | SCHEDULE

3 DAILY THRIVE ACTIONS
List the top 3 *to-do's* to get you closer to your goals.

_____

○ _____

○ _____

○ _____

_____

DAILY TASKS

DAILY TRIUMPHS

6 _____

7 _____

8 _____

9 _____

10 _____

11 _____

12 _____

1 _____

2 _____

3 _____

4 _____

5 _____

6 _____

7 _____

8 _____

DAILY NOTES

FRIDAY

AGENDA | SCHEDULE

3 DAILY THRIVE ACTIONS
List the top 3 *to-do's* to get you closer to your goals.

◯

◯

◯

DAILY TASKS

DAILY TRIUMPHS

6

7

8

9

10

11

12

1

2

3

4

5

6

7

8

DAILY NOTES

SATURDAY

AGENDA | SCHEDULE

3 DAILY THRIVE ACTIONS

List the top 3 *to-do's* to get you closer to your goals.

○ _____

○ _____

○ _____

DAILY TASKS

DAILY TRIUMPHS

6 _____

7 _____

8 _____

9 _____

10 _____

11 _____

12 _____

1 _____

2 _____

3 _____

4 _____

5 _____

6 _____

7 _____

8 _____

DAILY NOTES

SUNDAY

AGENDA | SCHEDULE

3 DAILY THRIVE ACTIONS
List the top 3 *to-do's* to get you closer to your goals.

○ _____

○ _____

○ _____

DAILY TASKS

DAILY TRIUMPHS

6

7

8

9

10

11

12

1

2

3

4

5

6

7

8

DAILY NOTES

WEEKLY REVIEW

STEP 1. BIGGEST TRIUMPHS / List your top accomplishments from the last week.

_____

_____

_____

_____

_____

_____

STEP 2. HOW FAR DID YOU GET ON YOUR 3 WEEKLY THRIVE ACTIONS?

_____

_____

_____

_____

_____

STEP 3. WHAT WORKED AND WHAT DIDN'T?

_____

_____

_____

_____

_____

STEP 4. MISSION STATEMENT REVIEW / Refer back to your _mission_. How well did you live out your _mission_ this past week? What do you need to do this week to better live out your _mission_?

_____

_____

_____

_____

_____

_____

"Weekly **reviews** help you reflect on your previous week. Weekly **previews** set you up for next week's success."

WEEKLY PREVIEW

VISION / Review your *vision* to help you remember what you want to accomplish in your six life domains.

QUARTERLY GOAL REVIEW / Write down the goals that you are focused on this quarter.

Goal 1: _____

_____

_____

   Next Action Steps:

   _____

   _____

   _____

   _____

Goal 2: _____

_____

_____

   Next Action Steps:

   _____

   _____

   _____

   _____

Goal 3: _____

_____

_____

   Next Action Steps:

   _____

   _____

   _____

   _____

WEEKLY PREVIEW

3 WEEKLY THRIVE ACTIONS / Write out the most important steps to help you move closer to your goals this week.

Action 1: _____

_____

_____

Action 2: _____

_____

_____

Action 3: _____

_____

_____

THIS WEEK AT A GLANCE / Write out any other personal or professional tasks that you have for this week.

PERSONAL

_____

_____

_____

_____

_____

_____

_____

PROFESSIONAL

_____

_____

_____

_____

_____

_____

_____

MONDAY

AGENDA | SCHEDULE

3 DAILY THRIVE ACTIONS
List the top 3 *to-do's* to get you closer to your goals.

_____

◯ _____

◯ _____

◯ _____

_____

DAILY TASKS

DAILY TRIUMPHS

6 _____

7 _____

8 _____

9 _____

10 _____

11 _____

12 _____

1 _____

2 _____

3 _____

4 _____

5 _____

6 _____

7 _____

8 _____

DAILY NOTES

TUESDAY

AGENDA | SCHEDULE

3 DAILY THRIVE ACTIONS
List the top 3 *to-do's* to get you closer to your goals.

○ _____

○ _____

○ _____

DAILY TASKS

DAILY TRIUMPHS

6 _____

7 _____

8 _____

9 _____

10 _____

11 _____

12 _____

1 _____

2 _____

3 _____

4 _____

5 _____

6 _____

7 _____

8 _____

DAILY NOTES

WEDNESDAY

AGENDA | SCHEDULE

3 DAILY THRIVE ACTIONS

List the top 3 *to-do's* to get you closer to your goals.

○ _____

○ _____

○ _____

DAILY TASKS

DAILY TRIUMPHS

6 _____

7 _____

8 _____

9 _____

10 _____

11 _____

12 _____

1 _____

2 _____

3 _____

4 _____

5 _____

6 _____

7 _____

8 _____

DAILY NOTES

THURSDAY

AGENDA | SCHEDULE

3 DAILY THRIVE ACTIONS
List the top 3 *to-do's* to get you closer to your goals.

○ _____

○ _____

○ _____

DAILY TASKS

DAILY TRIUMPHS

6 —
7 —
8 —
9 —
10 —
11 —
12 —
1 —
2 —
3 —
4 —
5 —
6 —
7 —
8 —

266

DAILY NOTES

FRIDAY

AGENDA | SCHEDULE

3 DAILY THRIVE ACTIONS
List the top 3 *to-do's* to get you closer to your goals.

6 _____

7 _____

8 _____

9 _____

10 _____

11 _____

12 _____

DAILY TASKS

1 _____

2 _____

3 _____

4 _____

DAILY TRIUMPHS

5 _____

6 _____

7 _____

8 _____

DAILY NOTES

SATURDAY

AGENDA | SCHEDULE

3 DAILY THRIVE ACTIONS
List the top 3 *to-do's* to get you closer to your goals.

○

○

○

DAILY TASKS

DAILY TRIUMPHS

6

7

8

9

10

11

12

1

2

3

4

5

6

7

8

DAILY NOTES

SUNDAY

AGENDA | SCHEDULE

3 DAILY THRIVE ACTIONS

List the top 3 *to-do's* to get you closer to your goals.

○ _____

○ _____

○ _____

DAILY TASKS

DAILY TRIUMPHS

6
7
8
9
10
11
12
1
2
3
4
5
6
7
8

272

DAILY NOTES

WEEKLY REVIEW

STEP 1. BIGGEST TRIUMPHS / List your top accomplishments from the last week.

_____

_____

_____

_____

_____

_____

STEP 2. HOW FAR DID YOU GET ON YOUR 3 WEEKLY THRIVE ACTIONS?

_____

_____

_____

_____

_____

STEP 3. WHAT WORKED AND WHAT DIDN'T?

_____

_____

_____

_____

_____

STEP 4. MISSION STATEMENT REVIEW / Refer back to your _mission_. How well did you live out your _mission_ this past week? What do you need to do this week to better live out your _mission_?

_____

_____

_____

_____

_____

"Weekly **reviews** help you reflect on your previous week. Weekly **previews** set you up for next week's success."

WEEKLY PREVIEW

VISION / Review your *vision* to help you remember what you want to accomplish in your six life domains.

QUARTERLY GOAL REVIEW / Write down the goals that you are focused on this quarter.

Goal 1: _____

_____

_____

Next Action Steps:

_____

_____

_____

_____

Goal 2: _____

_____

_____

Next Action Steps:

_____

_____

_____

_____

Goal 3: _____

_____

_____

Next Action Steps:

_____

_____

_____

_____

WEEKLY PREVIEW

3 WEEKLY THRIVE ACTIONS / Write out the most important steps to help you move closer to your goals this week.

Action 1: _____

_____

_____

Action 2: _____

_____

_____

Action 3: _____

_____

_____

THIS WEEK AT A GLANCE/ Write out any other personal or professional tasks that you have for this week.

PERSONAL

_____

_____

_____

_____

_____

_____

_____

PROFESSIONAL

_____

_____

_____

_____

_____

_____

_____

QUARTERLY REVIEW

STEP 1. BIGGEST TRIUMPHS / List your top accomplishments from the last quarter.

_____

_____

_____

_____

_____

_____

STEP 2. HOW FAR DID YOU GET ON YOUR GOALS THIS QUARTER?

_____

_____

_____

_____

_____

_____

STEP 3. WHAT WORKED AND WHAT DIDN'T?

_____

_____

_____

_____

_____

_____

STEP 4. MISSION STATEMENT REVIEW How well did you live out your mission this quarter? What do you need to do to better live your mission this next quarter?

_____

_____

_____

_____

_____

_____

QUARTERLY PREVIEW

STEP 5. VISION REVIEW

Your *vision* helps you remember what you want to accomplish within in your six life domains. Go to the *vision statement* pages of your new planner, answer the questions and then write out your *vision statement*.

STEP 6. REVIEW YOUR ANNUAL GOALS

Review your *annual goals* on pg. _____. Do you feel you need to make any changes? Rewrite your goals on the annual goals page of your next quarterly planner. Make sure to write all your goals for the year. Also, make sure to check the ones you have already accomplished, and write which quarter you are focusing on each goal. Fill in your *goal detail* pages of your next quarterly planner. It is important to rewrite this information in your new planner to help you stay focused on those things that will lead you closer to your *vision*.

STEP 7. PERFECT WEEK REVIEW

Go to the *perfect week* pages of your new quarterly planner. Are there any changes you need to make? If so, make the changes and fill in the perfect week of your new planner.

STEP 8. NEW DAILY PAGES

Go to the first two weeks of the *daily pages* of your new planner and fill in the dates for these first two weeks.

NOTES

NOTES

NOTES

NOTES

NOTES

NOTES

INDEX

	PAGE #

INDEX

	PAGE #

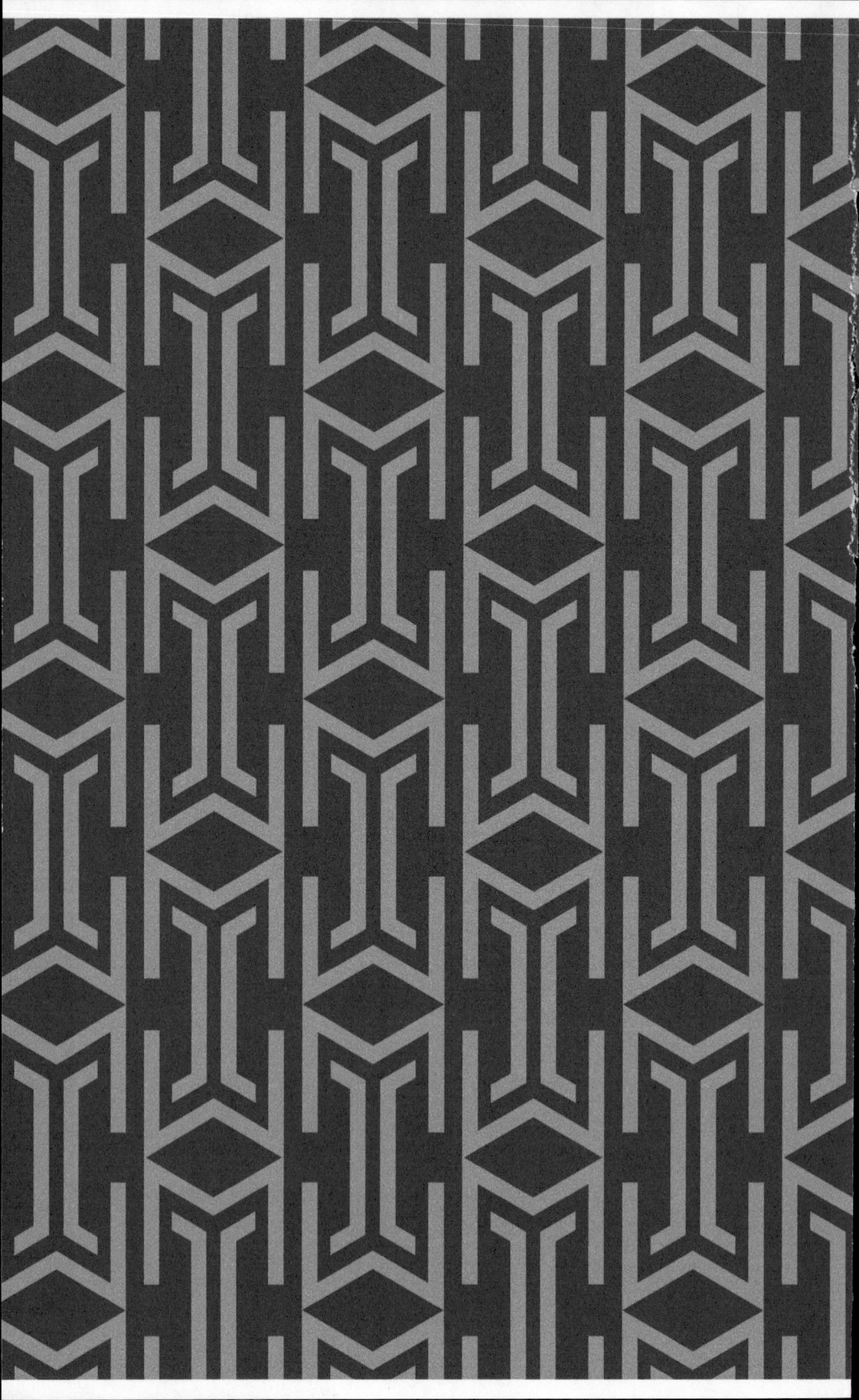